The World Beyond Today

By the same author
Adventure into Transformation
Ancient Memories, New Beginnings

The World Beyond Today

A Guide to Your
Multidimensional Future

Merriene Scott

with her spiritual messengers
from Illanitis

Published by Merriene Scott
Email: merriene@merrienescott.com

First published 2001
Reset and reprinted with minor amendments 2003
The World Beyond Today is the first book of a trilogy,
'Messages from Illanitis'.

National Library of Australia
Cataloguing-in-Publication entry

Scott, Merriene.
The world beyond today:
a guide to your multidimensional future.

ISBN 978-0-9751058-5-6
eBook: 978-0-9751058-8-7

1. Automatism. 2. Spiritualism.
3. Self-actualisation (Psychology). I. Title.
133.93

Typeset in 13/19 Bembo by Perth Editorial Service
Printed by Optima Digital Print, Perth
Cover mandala by Jen McCathie

This book is dedicated to my beautiful sons, Digby and Jamie,
who, with their enthusiastic attitude to life,
always encourage me to reach for the stars.

Contents

Acknowledgments

First and foremost I acknowledge the valuable support of my dear friend Annabelle Scanlon. She has generously and enthusiastically made time in her very busy life to work with me and, with my guides, transfer my handwriting onto the computer to create this book.

Grateful thanks to my valued friend and neighbour Irene Percy, who has always been very supportive and stepped in very efficiently to amend and complete the manuscript, and to Dr Janet Wale and Allan Watson for final editing and inspirational encouragement. To all my dear friends who have been there for me and supported this project in their own loving way, I have much gratitude.

Linda Jane Hearle, my loving thanks to you for encouraging me to finalise this project with confidence. Much appreciation to Jen McCathie, my friend whose passion for flower photography has provided me with the amazingly beautiful mandala for the cover.

Thank you to my serene, loyal mother Elsie, who listened with great patience to every page I wrote and read to her.

My beautiful sons, Digby and Jamie, with their enthusiastic attitude to life, always encourage me to reach for the stars.

My thanks to Dr Anne Russell (Brisbane, Australia), Helen Robertson, Darshan Carlson and Merriel Perrin (Perth, Australia),

Susan Newton (New York, USA) and Suzann Osborne (San Francisco, USA), all of whom gave their precious time to read the manuscript and have given me valuable feedback.

Much love and thanks also to my dear friend John, whose loving support from the world of spirit has been so very wonderful. Most of this manuscript was written in the months immediately after his 'death', and his cheerful words of advice were a lovely com- fort to me.

Last, but by no means least, thank you, reader, for selecting this book.

Preface

In the fleeting few moments between sleep and wakefulness I am always in a state of bliss. This is a most wonderful feeling, bridging the two worlds of dream and rational mind.

Since connecting with my spiritual guides, discovering more of my true self and journeying towards enlightenment, I am also able to be in this state of bliss much of my 'awake' time. You too can achieve blissfulness very easily, and this book will assist you to do that. The writing of this manuscript began with the discovery of my ability to write automatically. I have always had a fascination with the world beyond the three-dimensional, and was intrigued, having had my aura photograph taken, to see my spiritual guides as 'blobs' in the photograph. They were little round areas of magenta among the bright colours of the aura.

Being curious to know who my guides were and how to communicate with them, I found my way to automatic writing. This is a way guides can communicate with us, and provides a written record of the messages given.

It was on the night of the full moon on 9 September 1995 that I first tried my hand at automatic writing. It was approximately six weeks after a spiritual counsellor had told me I could. I had just had a lovely long shower and had talked with my spiritual guides by means of yes/no answers. This involved asking questions out loud and the answers were given to me as a backward rock for yes and a sideways rock for no. Although it was helpful, it was clearly very limited.

Picking up the little pad and pen next to my bed, I sat with my eyes closed and pen poised on paper, waiting. Nothing happened! Then I thought, perhaps I should ask a question. To my surprise the pen wrote NO (which is what I had hoped for as an answer). I asked another question, and received a YES answer. The third question was for a name, which was duly written. It was a long name and the pen ran off the little pad. This was completely enthralling. I slept really well that night.

The next night, realising I needed a bigger pad, I upgraded to an old A4 diary and repeated my attempts of the previous evening. The results were great - lots of words in between many squiggles and patterns. After a week I felt confident enough to demonstrate writing to my niece as I asked questions on her behalf. A few days later I repeated the process with a friend who herself asked the questions, and I wrote the answers.

I now use a sketchpad, and the writing has improved in clarity and flow, yet still with the words all joined together. Each day brings me further knowledge and closer communication with my loving guides and more understanding of universal wisdom.

During the subsequent time of writing for myself and others, I have explored so very much and have so much still to explore and learn of all that is in the world beyond the three-dimensional. I have discovered through my writing that my soul name is Merriene. I am now happily using this name in my role as a spiritual counsellor and writer; its vibrations resonate well with my essence. Previously I had been known as either Joan or Joanne.

After writing for about six months with my wonderful spiritual guides and very best friends, Hanka and Manilong, they asked me to buy a writing pad without lines for commencement of a book. As time went by and some of this manuscript had been written, they informed me that I was to have a change of guidance. The 'new' friends who came to join me and assist in my writing were Annaliese and then Marietta, guides and friends from many past lives. John, my beautiful friend and very close soul mate who had returned to spirit from the physical in 1996, also came to assist with the book. Hanka and Manilong had duties elsewhere, and I was now ready for a new level of under- standing and would benefit greatly with assistance from my 'new friends'.

So here we are. I do hope you enjoy the journey.

Perhaps you too will be able to communicate with your encouraging and supporting guides very soon.

Merriene Scott

Message from Spirit to Merriene

Have faith, trust and patience, and soon all will come forth. You are
but a servant of spirit and we have used you to write a message of
hope for the masses. Being such a simple book, many will read it
and find a way to live their life with new clarity and understanding.
The words are mystical magic, reaching deep within the reader
as he or she reads. Not only the words, but also the rhythm of the
words, will weave their desired magic and bring about the opening
of the heart.

We suggest, if possible, you read this book in quiet solitude for the message to be received and felt, from the words, their rhythm and metre.

The sometimes quaint sentence structures have deliberately been left as originally given and received.

You may perhaps experience a feeling of visiting other dimensions of yourself, where you are uplifted and transformed to a lovely state of being. Hold on to this feeling; with awareness and willingness you will soon be in this state more often.

Your heart will be open to receive and give love continuously and the upliftment will bring new joy to your life.

INTRODUCTION

A Message from Illanitis

Today is the first day of our new beginning. We are here to tell you where we are from and why we are here to help the planet at this time.

The planet is now going through some major changes as a home for the human race, and we are here to help the human race evolve to other dimensions so it is free from dependency on the Earth as its home. We are mainly from the place we will call Illanitis, and Joanne/Merriene has agreed to be our scribe for the information the planet needs to know now.

The place called Illanitis is far away in the cosmos and not known to many people on Earth. We are beings of light and love. Joanne is also from Illanitis and her soul is called Merriene; she will feel more comfortable with this name. To make life more enjoyable for her, we are to be with her each day and night and help her develop her spirituality to greater levels.

Can the world continue to exist as it is? We think not. It is now so polluted and fouled with much that is wasteful and unnecessary. During the next few years great changes must come, otherwise the planet will no longer be suitable for the human race to live on.

We are here to help those who are ready, and to encourage those who are not, to see the light and increase your understanding of your spiritual development. Those who are from the light are radiating out their love and light, and by example are influencing all those with whom they come in contact.

Can the planet survive another few years without the great changes that must happen? We do not think so. Can people on this planet understand what will happen to them if they resist change to the new way of being and thinking? Time is running out fast and, the more you live your lives with love, the more you will have a chain effect on many to help transform the masses who are living a life of decadence and destruction.

The masses are so unaware of where they are in the scheme of their lives. Their self-centred lifestyles are full of material needs and wants. They are so destructive to the planet and to the rest of humanity who are living simple, loving lives. Unless those masses are transformed by love and light to higher levels of spiritual evolution, and learn to respect their home, the planet Earth, their need to continue to live on it is debatable. Their return to spirit will be swift indeed, and many lessons will need to be learnt in the astral world before they can be invited back to this planet and enjoy the physical world again.

The urgency of the situation is of paramount importance to us. Our concern is very genuine, and we wish to help those who are eager to know about themselves and us. The masses are not interested in any more than where the next dollar will come from, or how they can improve their material world. How sad it is to be in such a state of being. We can give you much, much more. Many seek to know what their true path is during this lifetime, and spend much of their lives seeking it out. As time goes by we will progress to speak of many fascinating topics regarding the multidimensional future for all of you.

We now wish to explain what we mean by three-dimensional and multidimensional. Three-dimensional is a term for the physical world of most humans, with their use of five main senses. These are seeing, hearing, smelling, touching (feeling) and tasting. The sixth sense is also available, but rarely used, in the sense of intuition and knowingness. This sixth sense is the bridge to your multidimensional ability. Multidimensional is the ability to go beyond the five senses and to know and access other parts of yourself outside your so-called normal range. You can access your higher consciousness and link with universal wisdom, often called God. Multidimensionalism allows you to utilise all facets of your being and gives you your direct link with all that is – the creator of all life. We can explain this to you another way.

As you open up to your knowingness and intuition, your own guidance will become evident to you, possibly in the form of spiritual guides or teachers. These are other parts of yourself, which are linked to the universal wisdom. They are a connection between you and your own God/Goddess within.

The multidimensional future is coming rapidly, and the third dimension will no longer be all that is available to you. Can you now think about where you would like to be in your next lifetime? Do you want to return to a polluted Earth? The time has come to stop the situation becoming worse. We must move you to the light now and not delay.

Can the world do without fresh air and water? Can you go on without the material things you now enjoy? As you become multi-dimensional beings, material things will not matter to you as much. You will live more in the world of thought than the physical. You will enjoy many facets of being and the physical will become of less importance to you; and yet when you are in the physical, fresh air and water will be so very precious for you to have.

As you move from being three-dimensional beings to the multi-dimensional, many upheavals will occur on the planet. Already they have begun. Earthquakes seem to be happening more often, AIDS has struck down many and the wars of the world continue at an alarming rate.

To make sure you do not succumb to the evil of the world, we wish to assist you in your path to multidimensionalism. Those who are not open to the changes will be dealt with swiftly and leave the planet in many ways. The ways they will leave will be varied: earthquakes, fire, floods, disease, personal health problems and even suicide will be more prevalent. Many of you are very aware of the need for enlightenment and are eager to be shown the way. Many of you already know the way and only need some prodding.

The path to enlightenment is full of love and laughter. By discovering truth and light, you realise how wonderful the simple things of life are, compared to the difficult world of making money to survive and making money to impress others. It is a great relief, when the time comes, to give up all the trappings and just be. You do not need to do, just be, and the peace and contentment you have been seeking will be with you. We will help you to learn techniques to just be, and not confuse you with too many complicated words or instructions. Finding the inner you is the key to your realisation of who you are, and will help you gain your multidimensionalism, which is so very necessary for the future of the human race. Thank you for your decision to go on this journey with us into your multidimensional future.

CHAPTER 1

Showing You the Way

The human race, as it is now, has evolved from seemingly simple, unsophisticated beings. They managed to live simply, even though they developed clever ways to cope, with their methods of catching their food, providing shelter for themselves and their families, and developing herbal medicines and tools for their needs.

From that simple beginning, you have evolved to the complex, technically superior beings you are today. However, your understanding of why you are here has never been realised. Religions have played a major part in most of your daily lives, and on the whole have determined your methods of resolving your inner yearning for a reason for being. Those of religious zeal have taken control of many people's belief systems, and have told you how to believe and in what to believe. Much has been of great value and authentic. However much has been misconstrued from the actual truth, and all for the benefit of the religious powerbrokers, be it the priests or often politicians of the day.

Today, the shift away from religion and the church is growing, and many of you are seeking other ways of comfort and of finding answers to your growing restlessness within.

The time has come for humans to have a direct link with the universal wisdom, or God, by cutting out the 'middle man' who may currently control your relationships with the divine powers. As we help you to open up your own links to the universal wisdom, you will realise you no longer need to rely on anyone or anything else. The answers are all within you.

The universal wisdom is always available for you. All you need to do is ask and you will be helped. You can receive your own answers in your own unique way; you need no further churches or shrines at which to worship. Your shrine can be your own heart and your mind is your temple for knowledge.

As human beings you have mostly forgotten the memories of your past lives. As you are born each lifetime, your past memories are eradicated and you mostly spend the first few decades of your new life in complete oblivion of your true soul selves. Little children are very wise, and parents usually do not give them respect or credit for their wisdom. Gradually, as the child grows, the conditioning and beliefs imposed from the family they have chosen this lifetime will blot out their great memories gained from past lives.

In this new century there will be many changes on the planet. The world will be very different from the one you have known, and you need to adapt to the changes or not survive. We will assist you to adapt to the changes as they occur.

To begin with, we will be able to show you ways to nurture your soul and your spirit, as you also change your thinking. We will also help you to go about your daily work in a more positive and wholesome way. Your world will not be as materialistically orientated as it has been. The inner you will be an important part of your being, not the house you live in, the car you drive, the clothes you wear or the clubs you belong to. It will be your soul, how you think, how you feel and how you act that creates the cornerstones to how successful you are.

You will go to bed each night knowing that the day has been successful by the number of people you helped, the number of times you laughed and the number of times you helped others to laugh. It is not how much money you made, or how great a deal you signed up, or how many people you impressed.

You will be aware of many more intuitively aware people coming into your life as time goes on. When you are ready, someone will appear in your life just when you need them. We will guide you to the right people at the right time for you. You can then begin to tune into the many so-called coincidences that begin to happen in your life. It may be no coincidence when you read a book that you have been given by a friend or that you buy on impulse: you will have been guided to that book, as you need to know what it says. It may be no accident you are reading this book; it will be a special message for you, as you are now ready to begin on an exciting spiritual journey. The journey will be full of joy and wonder as well as practical advice.

Let us now begin to walk the road on this journey by taking the first step.

Changing Your Habits

To take the first step, we need you to be very clear in your intentions. Are you willing to let go of old patterns of being and to go beyond your comfort zone? Are you ready to stop watching so much television and to not read so many popular magazines? That is if you have not already done so.

Perhaps many of you are already very discerning in your television watching habits and selection of reading material. Did you know that television is a control of your senses and prevents you thinking for yourselves?

The vibrations exuded out from your television set are very harmful to your unique vibratory patterns. They distort them to such an extent that you can stop being your own unique self and become conditioned as if 'told' how to think, depending on the programs you watch. This is mass control of the planet via the powerful owners or directors of television channels. Can you imagine how easy it is for a few people to control world thought? It is time to stop this and for you to rise up and take control of your unique self. Collectively all of you can create a wonderful home here on this planet Earth.

Many of you already know that many magazines also act to think for you and tell you what is a good value and what is not. Many strange stories of people's lives are condoned; those unacceptable humans are not only made to look acceptable, but worshipped, as though how they live is the role model for everyone to follow.

The choice is yours. You have so many people of value to learn from and so many books of value you can read. Do you really wish to spend your precious life filling it up with information that is not worthy of your attention?

Please be discerning. It is your precious life and yours to do with as you wish.

If you are not already discerning, perhaps you can begin by turning off the television set in between programs you have selected to watch for the evening. Use the time in between when the television is off to go outside and look at the stars in the sky, walk the dog, talk to someone you love, or phone a dear friend. Talk about how they are feeling and not about things you or they are doing. You will be surprised how precious this time becomes for you, and how much richer and rewarding your life becomes.

Before long you will make choices about which programs are worth viewing and become more discerning in all you watch. Perhaps even later you may decide that your time is more valuable spent with people, or reading valuable information, rather than watching television at all. Time spent in the most positive way possible will result in a more positive life, and the rewards may then come to you when you least expect them.

Finding Your Life Purpose

We are keen to help you to understand that your life is very precious, and we encourage you to find your life purpose as soon as possible.

This will bring you greater contentment. To find your life purpose, it will be necessary for you to sit very quietly and meditate. You can meditate in many ways. Meditation is not as difficult as you may think. There is no single way of doing it, and whatever you do will be beneficial to you, so please try. The easiest way is to sit in silence early in the morning about dawn, before everyone else is up and about or before the phone begins to ring. Sit for about half an hour and blank your mind of your day-to-day worries. Just think of a lovely scene or hum some lovely music in your head. We are keen for you to know more about yourself, and this is the way to discover who you really are.

Another good way to meditate is walking or sitting by the beach, river, pond or stream, as the joining of the water and land is a very spiritual place. We are aware it is hard for many of you to do that, so you could use the shower with the water running over you. Unfortunately water and power bills always have to be taken into consideration; however we think it is worth the difference it can make to your whole being. Try it, and you will notice the difference in your tranquil state. You will be so much more centred and peaceful.

Another place to meditate (and contemplate) is in the country, where the trees, bushes and scenery are so beautiful. Just being there will enrich your whole being. Even being in a small garden, or making some other connection with nature, is a very powerful way to show your intention to connect with the divine and give recognition to who you really are.

Please meditate as often as you can on a regular basis because, as you do, the cumulative effect will begin to be evident to you. It is not what happens during the meditation but what occurs in your life each day.

The more often you meditate, the more pronounced will be the evidence in your daily lives. We do not expect you to be perfect with your meditations, and do not expect you to have an exact half hour each day. Do as much as you can fit in, even if it is only for a few minutes some days. It will keep your line of communication with us open, and we will know you are attempting to be with us always.

As time goes on you will begin to notice your life is flowing so much better. Favourable incidents will occur with much less effort. By that we mean you will meet people who are important to you much more easily. They will be there for you when you need them, the phone calls will come when you want them, and all will be positive and loving.

When difficult times arise, as they will, you will cope with them with much more ease and less stress.

We are not able to control your destinies; however we will be able to assist you to cope with whatever comes your way with much less trauma.

Detaching from Dramas

Another step in your journey to multidimensionalism is learning to detach yourself from the dramas in your life. The dramas that unfold are a part of living; however they are not really necessary and you can live more joyfully without them.

When next you have a drama unfolding before you, be the observer and observe from a distance if you can. Sometimes that is not possible, as you are in the drama. If that is the case, please do not react as you once did. Stay calm, listen to what is being said and then do not react. Allow the other person time to dwell on what they have just said to you; often they want your reaction immediately, and when you do not respond they lose their power and intention.

By remaining silent you will have averted drama. Wait and then respond, without taking on any of their anger. You can then speak rationally and quietly to them. Acknowledge what they have said and allow yourself time to think of what their intention is and what they have meant.

Dramas are not to be taken seriously, as they are just ways of others having power over you. You will soon be free of them when others realise you are not to be tampered with.

You will soon be centred, balanced and joyful, and no one will want to create a drama with you. They will feel secure and peaceful in your company. Your aura will be loving and full of happiness, and will affect the other person immediately they are in your presence; the path to multidimensionalism is full of happiness and love. You will not hesitate to improve your life as you proceed on this journey. The rewards are truly there for you, and they will come very quickly when you have begun on this journey towards the light.

Being Positive

Another step that will help you to eliminate your dramas is to be a very positive person all the time. Positive people are the ones who seem to have all the luck. It is not so. Positive people create their own 'luck'. They bring about lovely happenings as they have such attractive auras – all good is attracted to them.

You can bring good fortune to yourself by being positive at every opportunity. You will then see the results of your changed attitude. Begin immediately to do positive things for those around you. Give unconditional love to those who are not so nice to you, and so change their attitude to themselves.

As you become more positive in your daily life, you will notice the difference in how others react to you. You will be treated with respect and happiness, and those who are negative around you will disappear from your life. As you move on in whatever you are doing, you will have important happenings to bring your life into a greater state of respect and wholeness. This will not happen by accident. You will have created it for yourself. We all create our own circumstances, and you will have created your own lovely state of wholeness for yourself. The rewards will continue to come, and, as you move further on your journey, many delights await you.

The most important points to remember so far are to think positively, to not allow dramas into your life and to meditate each day. Also turn off your television sets as much as possible, and do not buy 'trashy' magazines. Do not allow others to tell you how, or what, to think or feel.

You are the master of your own destiny and, if you wish to fulfil your destiny as you have organised, you will be clearing the way for that to happen much more quickly and easily. Perhaps you now see what can be done to improve your life? If you do not wish to spend it asleep, by taking these steps you will wake up to who you really are and why you are on the Earth plane.

Living in the Now

The life of an enlightened being is fulfilling and joyful. Your journey to the light is not one of pain or suffering; you will float along and enjoy each moment. We suggest you live in the now.

To live in the past, or the future, is not worth worrying about. The past has gone and cannot be changed. The future is yet to be, and you create it however you wish by your thoughts now. The thoughts in the now will send out the message to the future of your intentions and desires, and you will be rewarded with them if you are positive in the now.

The moment at hand is all you have, and, if you do all you possibly can to make this moment fulfilling and joyful, the next moments will bring your karmic payback. Sometimes you do not know you are receiving your rewards until a long time afterwards, as the effects of a moment can take a while to take effect.

Being Fully Aware

The next step along the road to enlightenment is to be fully aware, aware of all those around you and aware of your own purpose. When you are aware of your own purpose for being on the Earth plane, you can achieve all you need to achieve relatively easily. Many people are not aware of their life purpose and, as we have said before, you can become aware by meditation and silence. You will then become very clear in what it is you want to do with your time here on Earth.

Your awareness is vital for you to achieve multidimensionalism. You will unblock the flow of goodness and positivity and move yourself forward in your state of being. Do you know why you need to be multidimensional? The reason is not apparent to most humans. You will be going from one state of existence so very soon in the scheme of things, and you need to be ready.

The human race is to evolve to other levels of being, and we encourage you not to stagnate at the level many of you have been at for so very long. The Age of Aquarius is truly a time of great changes, and they are already evident in many of the people who are enlightened.

The frequency of your media in reporting phenomena is increasing to the extent that it is now commonplace in your newspapers. Very soon the media will be writing more of these happenings and will treat them as normal news, not way-out fantasy. You can be part of the happenings about to occur.

When you are multidimensional, you will have access to your psychic powers and will know instinctively of things about to occur in the near future. You will also be able to see others' auras (energy fields), and know some of the things they are thinking about. You will be able to teleport to other countries just by thinking about where it is you wish to go, and also be able to talk with your family and friends who are back in spirit. Communicating with your spiritual guides and your intuitive (higher) self will be so very easy for you. These events will all be very natural to you after a while. You can also be aware of many other sensory pleasures, as your sense of smell, vision, hearing and feeling will be escalated to heights of awareness not previously known.

You may smell the perfumes of your guides, and see their forms in front of you. You may also be able to hear their voices and listen to their lovely music, when you are tuned in. We are around you all the time and wish to be able to communicate more fully with those of you who are ready, and are aware.

The earlier you begin your transformation, the quicker will be the rewards and joy you can have from your heightened state of being. You can do and be whatever you desire, if you have the intention and the confidence.

You may have opposition from many areas of humanity. There will be those who fear for you in what you are now doing, and those who fear for themselves in what you are undertaking. The fear of the unknown is very strong in many people and, as it is unknown, they will not try to understand at all what big changes you are taking to improve your life.

You need to be strong and single-minded in your approach to your work on changing your state of being. The 'knockers' will be all around you. They do not want you to change from the known person you have been to a new, unknown person. Little do they know that, as the new, unknown person, you will be more loving and joyful and have much more happiness and success in your life.

Now we must conclude this chapter by stating that we wish you joy and happiness in your steps towards your new you. You will find the rewards are wonderfully satisfying.

CHAPTER 2

The Planet as It Will Become

Improving the Environment

The planet is now on the verge of great upheavals if you, as the human race, do not take steps to change your ways. The way the world is changing, it will no longer be a fit place for you to enjoy your environment. The steps you can take to stop this happening are very important.

The first step is to stop polluting the Earth with your rubbish. The main culprits are of course big industries, with the fumes and rubbish they create along with whatever product they are producing. Governments need to be very strict in their guidelines to all industries and manufacturers. Of course when you exist only in the world of thought, you will not have any need to solve any of these problems. However, as these problems are very real to those here now, you must deal with them.

When the human race goes back to living more simply, the demands for all these products will be minimised and the slowdown will occur. Acid rain is now a huge problem in many areas of the world, fish are inedible and crops are very suspect in many countries.

Nuclear disasters have so polluted the environment in many areas that the human race is mutating to undesirable beings. You can assist to halt the pollution of the Earth by going to your local council and asking them for some recycling containers for you to put your plastic, paper and glass in.

We know many of you are already very aware of recycling, and are contributing very well with your efforts. You have all been so used to throwing everything out together, and not worrying whether they are to be saved or buried. Soon there will not be any room left to bury all your rubbish. So much can be saved and recycled again, stopping the continual chopping down of trees and manufacturing of more chemicals for products. Many councils already have wonderful programs being activated. Go and congratulate them and reinforce what they are doing by your enthusiasm.

The next step is to look at your own back yard so to speak. If each person has little rubbish and causes no pollution, that will have a multiplying effect on the world. It will create much more fresh air and visual enjoyment for you all. In your own homes, have a look at what is undesirable.

You possibly do not know what is a pollutant. Your refrigerator may well be, with all the carbon it produces. The new refrigerators are now carbon free, so, if you can, get rid of your carbon-producing refrigerator and buy a lovely pollutant-free one. Those of you who are feeling lucky to have a refrigerator at all must not become too worried by it. As time goes by you will create the wealth needed to be able to buy a new one. More about that later.

Also look at the ways you use to keep warm in winter. Do you have an open fire, or a wood-burning fire of some sort? If so, please take steps to make sure you do not send carbon gases into the atmosphere.

Many of the wood fires today are adjusted to remove the dangerous poisons before the smoke goes into the air, and are quite safe. Those of you who have open fires will have to make sure the wood you use is very dry and toxin-free, as certain types of wood are not suitable.

You may need to hunt around to find such suitable wood, and you may find you have to pay more for it. However the reward will come to you for your efforts. You will have the satisfaction of knowing you are not contributing to the poisons in the atmosphere. Your car is also a large distributor of pollutants into the atmosphere, so please ask your garage to check whether your car is expelling toxins. Unleaded petrol is now available in many countries and your car can be converted to receive this if it is not already. If everyone were to abide by these few simple guidelines the world would soon lose the threat of destruction.

Another step to avert the tragedy is to become aware of the many hazards already around you. Within your homes you have many vibrations intruding into your beings that are very destructive to your body. As we have mentioned, the television set is a source of subliminal control via what is being shown visually to you, and also what is being said.

Besides that, the electrical currents radiating from the set, when it is on, are disturbing your natural vibrations that are normally in tune and positive. The currents being radiated from the television distort your own vibrations, and so upset your harmony and joyfulness. The radio and microwave currents are similar in their distorting of your finely tuned waves.

The only positive medium you have is your music, as long as the music has vibrations of love and joy. Much music is also at odds with your own vibrations, and will make you nervous and exhausted. Be very selective with your music and you can then create a wonderful happy environment in which to live. Your own intuition will tell you which music is suitable and that which is not. Discard that which is not, and embrace all that is uplifting and beautiful for your spirit.

Improving Yourself Physically

The next step on your journey is a reminder to check what you are eating and drinking. Food is what you are – you are what you eat. The foods and drinks you consume will determine how you look and how you feel about yourself. The better the food is that you eat, the better it is for your brain and your entire body.

Also, your skin will react to what you eat. Your skin will glow if you are feeding it well, nourishing it both internally and externally. The skin is a great indicator of your state of health and the balance in your body. It is the largest organ of your body and is a wonderful barometer of all that is going on in your life.

It will reflect your emotions, feelings and state of health very accurately. Depending on the food you are consuming, your skin will tell you whether it is happy or feeling neglected. The best indicator of your state of wellbeing is therefore up to you.

Make the best choices you can in the type of foods you consume. These will vary depending on the type of person you are. If you are a very active outdoor type of person, your requirements will be very different from those of the type of person who stays indoors and does very little in the way of athletic pursuits. Also it will depend on your metabolism.

You are made very differently from each other, and you will need to determine whether you burn up your fuel quickly or slowly. You will know which type you are by thinking how quickly you put on weight if you consume the wrong foods too often. The important thing to remember is to be selective, by only eating what you need and not what you feel you want.

On the matter of eating meat and dairy products, we feel that is a very personal matter for you to decide. As mankind has nearly always been a meateating species we do not wish to condemn this habit; however it is not necessary for your survival to eat meat products. The many wonderful nuts and fruits available will supply all your needs, along with a variety of vegetables of every colour. Make sure you have a variety at all times and mix the colours, as they all have reasons for their different colourings, which we will discuss at another time.

Vegetables, fruits and nuts are a gift to mankind to nurture you, and provide what is needed to sustain your energy system. As time goes by, man will not need to eat at all. You will be sustained purely by the energy of the sun. You now always feel more energised when you have had a lovely sunny day and have spent some time soaking up the warm rays of energy from that source.

The sun will be a great provider of all your energy needs as the human race evolves to multidimensionalism. Make sure you take care in only eating food that is freshly picked, as that is still holding the energy of the sun and will pass it on to you.

Food that has been cooked or held in storage for quite a while will have lost its energy; it will not be as valuable to you. Eat as much raw, freshly picked food as you can. Shop if possible every few days, and only buy the amounts necessary for that amount of time. You will then reap the rewards of your thought and concern for your body, which is your vehicle for your soul in this lifetime, and must be given much respect. The fresh air you breathe in deeply is also very important, as it contains the oxygen so very necessary to vitalise the body's organs. Most humans breathe so lightly they do not refill their lungs completely, or often enough, to continuously feed the body with fresh supplies of oxygen.

The body is very important to help you achieve that which is your purpose in this lifetime. The more respect given to your vehicle, the easier will be your task. Make sure you do not abuse it with alcohol or drugs (including coffee, tea and soft drinks that contain caffeine), as you will then no longer be in control of your destiny. That right will be gone and you will not achieve what it was you came here to do. Small social amounts of alcohol are acceptable, as the alcohol is a relaxant and may assist you in becoming more who you really are at times. Many of you are teetotallers and we applaud your decision to be free of all drugs or related products. It will be strange for you to think of a time when you no longer need to shop for food, prepare food or have to eat at all.

The consequences will be very devastating for those who produce the goods you eat, and the planet will evolve very differently when that time comes. The changes will come very gradually and those producers will gradually shift their focus to other ways of making a living. This will happen over many generations. When the time comes to exist without food, the human of the future will not have any need to spend so much valuable time on the process of eating and cleaning up afterwards. The social aspect of dining will be a thing of the past and you as the human race will find other means of indulging in social interaction. Your consumption each day of plenty of pure water will keep you very healthy, by eliminating toxins easily from your body.

To help you speed up your journey toward multidimensionalism, we strongly recommend you eat only pure raw vegetables and fruit. You will feel light and energised without the heaviness of meat and animal products in your body. You will wish you had taken these steps many years ago. We must also add, grains and nuts are very essential to your wellbeing, and a valuable part of your daily diet.

The beginning of your new life will begin as you understand what you are to do now you are becoming multidimensional. As the world changes, so will you. You can begin to look forward to each day as an exciting opportunity for incredible happenings. Each meeting with someone of importance to you will be no accident. Exchange of ideas or information will occur, which will be very beneficial for you to act on. Many new people will come into your life and you will have a lot of new opportunities given to you. You must decide for yourself which of these opportunities are valid for you, and then act on them.

If you keep being presented with the same opportunity over and over, you certainly are meant to act on that particular one. Each opportunity will be another step along your future path, and, as you act with awareness and positivity, so will the path before you be lit even more brightly. The way of the future for you will become easier and brighter.

We certainly do not promise it will become easier in a hurry, as you need to be very dedicated to your cause and work on it continuously. There is no easy road to enlightenment, and you cannot just wake up one morning and declare you are now truly enlightened. It will be slow and steady, and you will not notice the very day you are really there.

Seeing What You Need to See

The next step towards your future lies in your ability to see what it is you need to see, and not to be sidetracked by all the tempting deviations that will be put before you.

Do not allow others to tempt you from your path. It will happen often, and those who tempt you will not understand what it is you are achieving. They fear for themselves that they may be losing a friend or relation to some strange way of being, and not wish that to happen.

Your own quiet determination to be true to yourself, and do what you need to do, will be a great asset to you during your difficult transition time, especially in the early stages. The wonderful thing about your transition will be the way you meet up with others, seemingly quite by chance, who are also on the same path as you are. They will give confirmation that you are not alone in your new direction.

Before long the way will be full of many others taking the same journey, and you will no longer feel alone along the path to enlightenment and multidimensionalism. As time goes on, you will realise it is those people who are not on the path who are in the minority, and you will gently be able to try to persuade them to take a look at some of your ideas and thoughts.

Love

Another very important task for you to do is to make sure you are continuously giving love to all you encounter. Love is the only reality we really have, and with love so much can be accomplished. Give love even to those who are not your favourite people.

With the receiving of unconditional love they will, without understanding why, feel so much better about themselves, and then hopefully act with more love themselves the next time you see them. Love is allencompassing and very satisfying in all relationships you have, be it between two adults in an intimate relationship, between parents and children, other family members, friends, acquaintances, pets, or even with the plants in the garden.

With love so much can happen positively for all concerned, and the benefits are enormous. Without love, the energy is drained from the particular area where love is not received, and the person, animal or plant concerned will wither and eventually die. As we are all made of energy, we need to receive loving energy to operate successfully at all times. Love can be such a wonderfully easy property to give. It is not like material property, and costs nothing in money terms yet gives so much more in value to the person receiving it. The intentions when giving love are so very pure, and we must also know how to receive love in a gracious way; that is why the love is given. The receiving of love is a very important aspect of the giving of love. If the receiver does not acknowledge the giver, the giving will lose its intention and so will not create the effect that was meant in the beginning.

To receive a gift or compliment with much enthusiasm is very important in the scheme of love; unrequited love is wasted energy. Your time is valuable to you and we want you to be careful as to whom you give your love, even though unconditional love is the aspect of love that can be given to everyone, always.

The love we mean you to be discerning with is the love you give conditionally, the love you give in special relationships with your friends and partners. Then you must choose wisely and not love just for love's sake. The other person must earn your love and you must earn theirs.

We consider that many people are lonely and need companionship. A co-dependency relationship is not needed though, and much thought must be given to relationships based on this type of companionship. We are very aware many of you will not need to go out seeking love, as you have learnt to love yourself; you will be very independent, whether or not you are married or have a partner, and lead a very satisfying life.

The aspect of love called conditional love is a very strong aspect of all human lives and is essential to bring forth a completion to your soul's journey. Many people do not have satisfactory love lives, as you may call them, as they live in fear of giving of themselves to another person. They do not want to risk being hurt, or risk revealing who they think they are. They therefore live lives of isolation without risking loving another, in case they are rejected or exposed for who they are.

Everyone needs to be loved and everyone needs to share their lives. Humans do not undertake their journeys to the physical world to live in complete isolation. Those who do not choose to have at least one loving relationship with someone are not fulfilling their reason for being. The love you receive from others is very important to your soul.

As you move through your life you need to receive love continuously to be energised and nurtured. Without love your soul will die. You may go through life without many clothes or nourishing food; however if you are being loved, you will be sustained and will be able to cope with whatever you are faced with.

Those who are not in a loving environment will not sustain balance in their lives and soon become ill and do not last. Love is the greatest nurturer of all, along with energy from the sun. That is all you really require; love and energy. You can achieve anything you desire if you are sustained with both of these.

Self-love is only achieved with wisdom, which little children have. As they are, however, conditioned by the environment in which they grow, they lose their wisdom and adopt behaviour patterns imposed on them by their parents and others.

Some very fortunate children have parents who are wise and self-loving, and the little ones retain their wisdom; they are full of self-love from their birth until they leave the Earth plane. How wonderful if all of you had this same start to your lifetime.

Most of you have to work hard as you mature to regain your wisdom and memories of past lives. Then, as you remember who you really are, you can give your love much more freely, because you are uninhibited by your doubts.

As your confidence grows, so does your love of yourself, warts and all. You realise you are meant to be as you are, and should not wish to change the shape of your nose, your height or the colour of your eyes. You are perfect as you are, and will achieve your mission here on Earth by believing in yourself as well as using your abilities and unique gifts to their full advantage, to benefit mankind.

You all have unique gifts, and have been blessed with these gifts to be used to help others in their quests to find theirs.

Do not ignore your gifts, as you will be wasting this lifetime if you do. If you do not know your own gifts now, we will help you find them. The quicker you begin to realise the real reason you are here, the quicker your life will begin to flow more smoothly, and the path forward will be lit for you to follow.

We cannot stress too emphatically how much we want you to find your true path and to step on to it as soon as you can. Many do not follow their true path and end up ill, or unhappy with what they are doing; the environment in which they are living can be very wrong for them. Their whole life becomes a futile exercise, and they will need to come again to achieve what it was they came for this time.

Being Authentic

When you have found your true path, the next step is to make sure you are truly being authentic. Being authentic means being really true to yourself, and not telling people one thing when meaning something else. You must realise that the truth at all times is paramount. When you are truthful all the time, you are living proof of what and who you really are.

Those who know you will be very happy to be in your energy space. Your truth will radiate from you as you project your own knowingness. You will be able to glow with wisdom, peace and joy. Others will be magnetically drawn to you.

They will then also glow and feel good about themselves in your company, and seek you out more and more. The magnetism you project will become infectious, and those who you touch will then touch others. You become a beacon of light to all who stand near you. Your authenticity will become natural to you.

It will then be hard to go back to putting on a facade for certain occasions; you may decide to 'risk' being authentic continuously. You may feel you have to be 'brave' to do this, and may perhaps find it hard to begin with. Before long you will know it is the best way to be at all times. To be authentic is such a relief to you after many years of believing you should be the person others think you are, or ought to be.

You think you must behave a certain way to gain approval, or look a certain way to be accepted in a certain group or culture. If you do not feel comfortable looking or being a certain way, just stop and consider how you do like to dress or act. Be as you wish, not as you feel others wish you to be.

The freeing up of your identity will have a liberating effect on your soul, and your true self will begin to emerge from behind the persona, this strange person you may have been for many years and have learnt to cope with, even thinking that was the real you.

Others will, when they get used to the real you, secretly wish they could be as brave as you have been. They may try to emulate your decision to rid yourself of the shackles of your former persona. How very wonderful it will be when we can know a person we meet is their true self. Today is to be the first day of your beginning to discard all that you do not like about yourself. Show the world who you really are.

You will have so much fun discovering for yourself your true identity.

Now take note of all you have learnt so far in the messages conveyed here. If you have actually begun to practice what we have told you, you may be beginning to notice changes happening in your life. As you now have an intention to change, your guides will be speeding up their help to you and events will happen that have great significance to you. Your life will begin to flow at a better rate, a smoother path is ahead for you and you begin to experience more joy and laughter. Are you feeling this way already? We do hope so. The more truthful the intent you have to become multidimensional, the faster will be the change for you. We are very eager for you to arrive at this glorious state as soon as you can, as then the planet will survive, even if it is in another form to that which it is in now.

You can all assist in what must be with your eagerness for transformation. The planet will then continue to be a home for the human race.

CHAPTER 3

The Way Forward

The way forward for you now will not be so difficult. As you are well on your exciting journey, you will feel much satisfaction in what you are achieving.

You will be looking more healthy and cheerful; you will have a sparkle in your eyes and a glow to your skin.

Your mind will be more alert and not cluttered with useless information. You will be more loving to all you are in contact with and you will have abundant energy.

Don't worry if you need more sleep initially, as this is our way of accessing your soul. You are back in your true soul state during your sleep, and you are also accessing your own eternal wisdom.

Do not think you are being lazy if you sleep longer than normal. Just embrace it and acknowledge what is happening for you.

Where You Go After Physical Death

Can you now begin to think of where you go when this life is over? You may not know where, and we can help you understand where it is you are going after death. You do not just disappear, as you may think. You are not that easily disposed of.

Before you die, the etheric matter prepares for your departure, even though you may not be aware of this and have no knowledge of your impending 'death'.

Many people do have a sense of what is to happen, and take time to make plans in advance so as not be taken unawares when their time arrives. It is very easy to make arrangements, if you so wish, once you are aware of signs.

You may notice that you are much more detached from everyday affairs and do not have as many worries as normal. You may also have a sense of great joy and peace about you, and will be so happy with everyone, wishing them great happiness and joy also.

You may ask why does it matter where we go after death, as it is of no concern to you. We think it matters a great deal, as being in the physical is only a very small portion of your reason for being.

You are a spiritual being having a life in the physical so as to have very valuable experiences. When you leave your physical body, your etheric matter helps your soul to return to where it came from before you were born. You were born into a particular body for a particular purpose.

You were the one who decided why you needed to come this time, and only you know when the time is right to leave again to return to the astral world.

The astral world is a simple term for all that is, other than the physical world. It really has many, many dimensions and layers, so to speak. You return to that area from whence you came, and then sort out if you have earned the right to move on to greater things.

You will be very clear in your intentions when you arrive 'back in spirit', and soon realise if you achieved what it was you came to the physical to do. There will be a revision of your life on the Earth plane.

You may then go back to areas of the Earth plane to make amends where you may have disappointed others, or done some wrong to them.

You can then assist them as a guide and make their life a much happier one. If you have achieved much and were kind and loving, you will be rewarded with a higher-level environment in which to continue your work.

You may wish to go back to the physical very quickly, or you may wish to stay and work on the astral level for some time. The choice is yours, and you will know which choice to make.

Those of you who have done much spiritual work and are very enlightened may wish never to return to the Earth plane. You can achieve more by working from the high realms, and be of great assistance to many, by remaining in spirit.

When you die you are not alone on your journey back to the astral plane. You are guided by your own loving spiritual guides, who have been with you always and will assist in your return to spirit with ease. You will not suffer at all, as the pain is left behind, and you will find yourself feeling absolutely wonderful and free. It is a great experience, once the decision has been made to return to spirit.

You will not be very welcome, though, if you return when you have not stayed as long as you originally chose to. Suicide is not a good solution to your problems on the Earth plane, and you will need to return to the physical again, repeating all you have just experienced so as not to opt out of the conditions you have chosen to learn from.

Communicating With Spirit

By this time in your new level of being, you may be experiencing your own communication with your spiritual guides. They are anxious to communicate directly with you as soon as possible.

This may happen for you in a variety of ways. You will have one or more gifts, either visual, auditory, intuitive thought or feeling, or maybe writing. When your gift has been revealed to you, either by your own perceptions or through the help of someone who is already multidimensional, you can explore many areas of your own unique reason for being on the Earth plane at this particular time.

You are all gifted and able in one or more ways to have your own channel to your guides and the universal source, and be empowered with the glory of the universe.

The wonder of your own special being is revealed to you by your own connection. When this happens, your life will never be the same again.

You will be amazed and thrilled with what is now available to you. So by now we can hope you are beginning to see where it is you are going. You are now reaching another more wonderful existence that encompasses the levels of awareness that were not available to you a little while ago. With much dedication and enthusiasm, you will certainly be able to cope with all that is given to you to deal with in this lifetime.

Nothing will be too much for you to handle. With your new state of awareness, your calmness, centredness and joy, your perceptions of your so-called problems enable you to tackle everything with great ease. When dealing with the essence of the particular problem before you, let go of your attention to it and trust that the universe will re-solve the small details in its own way.

Helping Others

The next step in your multidimensional awareness is to be able to convert your new state of being into going out in the world and helping others.

You can help them to see what it is they need to do to make their lives more fulfilling. Please do this by example only, and do not try to convert them into your way of looking at things.

All you can do is tell them what it is you have been reading and how you have been exploring with your thinking and altering your living habits.

If they like what they see, they may then decide to investigate what it is that is making you look and act so very happy.

As you go along in this new world of yours, you will not be worried by the things that worried you before. Your days will float by and you will see beauty in everything. The sunsets and sunrises will appear more beautiful, the trees will seem to talk to you, and animals and birds will be attracted to you easily.

Your aura will be large and beautiful and people will be drawn to you immediately, without knowing why. Their instinct for knowing you as a radiant being will be with them, and they will feel safe and energised by you.

The more positive you are, the more positive things happen to you.

Celebrating Each Moment

The next event you need to attract to yourself is the event of the celebration of life as it is this very moment. As we have said before, you cannot bring back the past or project your will into the future: all you have is this very moment.

Celebrating each moment will create so much positive karma, you can enjoy all that is before you. Do you have a problem with that? We know many of you have very stressful situations with which to cope in your life. You cannot avoid them, and we do understand that not every moment is joyful and happy. If you can deal with each moment with authenticity and good intention, your moments of joy will come.

Your celebration of the now is very important, and as you are doing that your future will unfold before you with effortless ease. We will tell you more about your future, even though living in the now is the only time you have.

Tests

The way ahead will be full of tests for you – small tests and really enormous ones. We will see if we can trust you to do what we know is in your best interest, and also test you to see if you trust us at all times.

They will come in all forms, and many will pose riddles of situations. You will have to work out the solution to each riddle. Much will be in the form of mind games, to see your reaction to a set of situations or circumstances. When you satisfactorily discover the answer to your riddle, you will then advance to more appropriate situations for you. This will be a reward for your new state of awareness. As your awareness grows, so will your state of multidimensionalism.

Do you now understand where you are to be in the next little while? The world as you have known it will be no more. As you become multidimensional, the energies of the world will vibrate very differently and you will respond accordingly.

The three-dimensional world will only be a small part of your existence. As you change, you can have far greater access to all that there is waiting for you to experience.

The far corners of the world will be easy for you to visit in your 'teleporting'. Hot and cold climates will have no effect on you, as you will be protected by new energy layers and vibrations that stop you feeling the effects of weather changes.

Your body shape will change according to the vibrational field you have entered. You can have great fun doing mischievous things with other vibrational fields and mean no harm of course.

As you are adapting to these changes, you will be able to notice them progressively becoming more radical and distinctive in their meaning. All you need to do is continue with your trust in what is happening, connect with your guides on a regular basis, meditate, be authentic and loving, and stay positive with everything that is happening to you.

Your awareness of every small change will help you to go on your path at a very fast rate indeed.

We suggest you now make sure you are very clear in your intentions of why you are on this spiritual journey. Ask yourself the following questions, and see what your answers are by listening to your heart.

Why do you wish to become multidimensional?

Why do you wish to change from the comfortable existence you may have already in the three-dimensional world?

Is it because you are restless and know there is more to your life than you already know?

Is it because you have had psychic experiences in the past and you have denied them or blocked them out for a long time?

We know many of you fear change, and are not prepared to step out of your comfort zones until you are pushed.

You may have been catapulted from your safe, cosy lifestyle by the end of a marriage or the death of someone very close to you. Usually this terrible disaster in your life has been planned since before you were born. It is part of your blueprint, so to speak: a set of circumstances that occur to help you learn very valuable lessons and search for more meaning to your life. It is only later, when you have gone through the trauma, that you can look back and see it was a turning-point in your life. You can then be thankful for having had that experience presented to you.

Acknowledging Spiritual Guidance

May you please consider the other side of the coin? Your guides are with you continuously, and are there to help you evolve to the highest level of spirituality you can achieve in this lifetime.

Can you not see how delighted they are, when you finally wake up to the knowledge that you have these wonderful helpers in your life?

The simple fact of acknowledging their presence is the greatest step you can take to begin your journey. From the moment of recognition and acknowledgment, everything is so much easier for your guides. They can work with you much more effectively now they know you are wanting to communicate with them at all times.

From the choices you have, they make it much easier for you in your decision-making. There is much celebration and joy when that time comes for you to have awareness of their presence in your life.

We trust you feel so much more comforted to know you are not alone and you have your loving guides with you at all times. Some guides are with you from birth, while others come and go as you need them.

At special times you may need extra guides to assist you, when you have exams or sickness. We are always available for you and help you with much love.

The time to make your decision to be a new type of person is right now. Do not procrastinate. Allow yourself to have courage to begin immediately.

The sooner you begin, the sooner your feelings will confirm that you have made the only decision you could have made. There is no going back. Many who fear the new way of being are beginning to question what it is they must do to go along with their decision. Before long you will be the one who is admired for all you stand for. Oh how wonderful to be so courageous and then to see how content you are becoming. Others' incredulity will be complete when you are the one who seems to be having all the luck going your way and opportunities presented to you.

Before long they will decide to have a little look at your ways of looking at life, and decide that perhaps they can begin the journey themselves.

Teleportation

We talked earlier of your ability to travel to other parts of the world at will; we call this teleporting or mind travel. Your ability to go from one time zone to another will come easily to some of you, once you understand that time does not really exist as you know it, and you transcend the three-dimensional existence to move to multidimensional ways of being.

You can then slip from your time in threedimensionalism to wherever you wish, just by closing your eyes and thinking of where it is you desire to be. You can be there in astral body and mind in a flash; your body in the three-dimensional reality will appear to be asleep. Your time can easily be spent elsewhere. The ability to learn about other cultures and peoples will be easy for you, as that is what you can be experiencing whilst you are travelling. As you teleport you cannot have any effect on the place you go to. You can only be an observer of all that is there and gain wisdom to help you back in your own reality.

We wish to warn you not to use teleporting as a way of opting out of the responsibilities you may have in the third dimension, as that is not the purpose of this skill.

Having respect for all you are now able to experience is of utmost importance, and we are very wary of those who have the wrong reasons. Your experiences with your newfound abilities will be exceedingly beneficial in assisting the many peoples of the world who are in great distress and need help to resolve vexing problems. When you are asked to assist somewhere in the world, you will be called upon and can be with the person and problem in a very few seconds if need be. The calls will come to your attention in many ways, as you are all unique in the way you develop your multidimensionalism. Do not become anxious about it now, as you must be fully enlightened and well prepared in other ways also before your services are called for.

Would you like to attempt teleporting before we go any further?

Please meditate to achieve a very peaceful state of being. Make sure you are very comfortable and will not be disturbed. Close your eyes and project your thoughts to the destination of your choice. Continue to think of this place. Visualise the scenery and the people and continue to visualise them for as long as necessary for you to make the leap in consciousness from the third dimension to the dimensional reality required for you to be actually where you have visualised.

To you it will appear as in a dream state; however everything will be much clearer and more rational, and the colours will be beautiful. You will also hear noises and smell all the things as you do in your own reality. Those in this place you are visiting will not be able to see or hear you. You will be an observer only, much like we guides are to most humans who are not enlightened. The roles are reversed, and you will be able to comprehend our position with you before you began on your path to multidimensionalism. We hope you enjoy the experiences you have.

To return to your own place again, take your thoughts there and return when you so desire. Just remember to thank your guides for helping you to achieve your newfound awareness and abilities to explore other places and other dimensions.

CHAPTER 4

The New Beginning

Clarifying Your Life Purpose

The new beginning of the Age of Aquarius is now here with you.

As you progress on your journey of enlightenment, you will become aware of your different perception of everything. Your feelings will be much more acute regarding what you wish to achieve with your time on the Earth plane.

You will know with more certainty what your purpose is for being here. The following points may help you to understand what your purpose is, if you have not found it by now.

The need to assist others in their paths to enlightenment will be paramount to many of you. Are you amongst these people?

Do you have a unique gift of healing or counselling others? If so, you will need to pursue that very quickly, as many will need your services soon.

Are you a good organiser of events and can you handle money matters well? Money will still be needed in the early stages of change. If so, your talents will be invaluable to assist in organising the state of being which is soon to occur.

Are you a compassionate human being who cares about your fellow man? If so, you will be needed to care for many who become lost and disorientated if they are to be saved in the future.

Sit quietly and think to yourself which of these points apply to you.

You will possibly have noticed all points may be your strengths, and so you may need to use all your gifts for the betterment of mankind as time goes on. As we have already discussed, the world will be a vastly different place in a few years' time, and you will be wise to be ready for the changes that are coming rapidly.

Once you have realised what your gifts are, you can proceed with life confident that you are on your true path. As this happens, please trust all will be well for you.

Trusting Yourself and Universal Wisdom

Trust in yourself and trust in universal wisdom within. This is paramount for you to receive all the help you need on your great journey.

The journey will be full of tests and obstacles, as we have already said, and as long as you continue to trust all will be well you will safely continue on your journey. When trust is lost, you will receive little reminders of what life would be like if you do not follow your true path. We do not say the journey will be easy; however it will flow much better for you with trust.

The more trust and faith you have, the quicker will be your time along the road to enlightenment. Arrival will be a really joyous event. You will not realise you have ended your journey until much later.

In retrospect you will look back to your last set of trials or tests and know you are finally through them all. You can set about helping others through theirs. The next time you are in the middle of a test, ask yourself:

Why is this happening to me?

Am I now learning another big lesson? How should I react to this situation?

The more thought you give to the problem at hand, the quicker it will be resolved. Also, if other people are involved in the problem, if you can continue to give them unconditional love and respect for their perspective on the situation, the sooner the test will be over for you.

The beginning of your future existence will be profoundly different from all you now know, and those of you who are ready will find the change remarkably easy. Those of you who are not prepared for the great change will be left 'behind' on the Earth plane as it now is, and not notice any difference. The enlightened ones will go beyond this third dimension to new dimensions of being, easily adapting to the more expansive opportunities available.

Those left behind will continue with their lives and have great difficulty in coping with the forces of evil they may encounter, as the world as they know it will not be a pretty or loving place. What a shame they do not listen to those from the light who show them the way to a new beginning.

It is all there for them if only they will take the time to investigate what it is all about. The time now is very critical for helping as many of you as we can to make the switch from the level of existence you are now in to the new level of being – the level which is full of love, light and joy.

Loving and Caring Thoughts

We now wish to tell you more about what it is you need to do to be prepared for your time in this new level of existence. You need to bring nothing with you except yourself, your love and creative thoughts. Your thoughts are all that will matter in this new existence of yours, so you can forget about your material possessions and all your work problems.

As long as you have loving and caring thoughts, you will be very successful in all you do. The future will be full of think tanks and thought exchange. You are now in that state a lot of the time with your computers and the Internet, as you call it.

The telephone also is only thought transference, with the voice as the method of communication for that. With the thought channels you have, you can create very powerfully all you wish for. Even now, if you think positively you have positive things happen for you. Vice versa when you think negatively.

Fear and Control

Much of what operates in your world today is based on fear. Fear is the opposite of love. Fear is such a powerful thought process it has kept most of you in a position of being controlled by the laws of the land and not by the love of your fellow man.

Can you not see the difference, when all thoughts of love could transform the world into a place for peaceful, joyful coexistence, with no need to fear anyone or anything?

The polarisation of those filled with love and those filled with fear is very obvious.

Many of you caught in the middle will need to make up your minds very quickly as to which way you are to go. Do you choose love or fear as your basis for living? It is as simple as that.

Many of you made the decision long ago to follow your heart, and love wins out continually. You are truly wonderful souls who will now have your rewards as you move towards the light and the new multidimensional world for you.

We are here to help you with your transformation and you will be guided continuously to follow your true path towards your new beginning. We are so delighted you are here with us, as you will take a huge leap forward towards enlightenment with what you are discovering now.

Can you continue to talk with all you meet about what you are now learning and experiencing? As we have said before, you cannot talk others into doing what it is you are doing. All you can do is show them by example.

Encourage them to read this book and it will help them to understand their choices. You may be surprised how grateful they are to you for showing them a way out of their dilemmas, why they are on the Earth plane and all the questions associated with that question.

The Astral World of Thought

We must make it clear to you where you have been before you arrived here in the third dimension, as mentioned earlier when talking about where you go when you die. Prior to your arrival on the Earth plane, your time was spent in the astral world of thought.

Depending on your level of enlightenment, you were on a level of the astral plane suitable to where you were in the scheme of things. This includes the number of lives you have already had, the amount of learning you achieved during those lives and your continuing development whilst in the astral state.

You would have achieved much work during your last time in the astral state. To learn certain very important lessons through all your experiences, you have chosen to return to the physical world. You chose the parents and conditions your circumstances most needed to learn the lessons necessary for you this lifetime.

You may have chosen to learn about love, hate or needing to let go, or a multitude of other issues we have all needed to experience to become true enlightened beings. The way is never easy, even if you have been blessed with wonderful parents and been brought up in a peaceful country with much abundance around you.

The issues with which you need to deal will come, or have already come to you. You cannot escape the tests and experiences you need, and if you do you will be confronted with them again and again until you deal with them and achieve your lessons, and become closer to understanding the nature of existence.

As you are tested so very many times, you will wonder whether it is worth going through all of what you are for your evolution. You will need to be strong and committed to all that is happening to you. As we said, the way will not be easy and, although you will hesitate to agree with us, your rewards will be fantastic at the end of it all, and you will then understand what we meant by everything that has happened to you.

We do hope you can be strong and determined to evolve, no matter what happens to you on your journey to enlightenment.

Meditation is the very best way to resolve so much of ones problems. It will help you become centred and grounded for what you need to achieve. Awareness of your position and those around you will also speed up your clarity of thought and purpose.

We are here to help you as the human race goes on to the next steps in your evolution. You are very necessary in the scheme of things to help that happen. Together we can go far in changing the state of the world, as you now know it to be.

With your own guides' help and much collective thought, the love in the world will expand to cover the whole atmosphere of the Earth plane. As it does so, the world will be healed of the many injustices that are happening to you and your close ones.

The negativity of those unenlightened ones will evaporate as they are enveloped with love and light from all those of you who have gone forth and developed around you your beautiful cocoons of love and light.

The energy field will be so expanded it will join up everywhere, and exclude the negativity from entering again. The wonder of it all will be when you can see what you have achieved with your positivity and love for all mankind.

The way to your new beginning is in your hands and thoughts. The sooner you continue to face all your hard decisions with love and knowledge of the outcome, the more rapidly you will proceed along the path of enlightenment.

CHAPTER 5

The Days of Change Are Now Coming

Changes to Your Body

Change is about to affect every one of you, as you become multidimensional. The changes will be both covert and overt, as you do not realise you are changing internally. You will only be aware of the external changes to you, and the world will be perceived differently as you go through your changes.

The internal changes will be quite major, although unknown to you at the beginning. Your brain will be quite different structurally as you open up psychically, opening to channel your own information.

We can then access you at all times and help you intuitively to know what you need, and to know how to act or react in situations. Also your heart will be so much more open and loving to all experiences you have, and we can pour our love in to you with greater ease.

You may feel tingling all over your body more often, and also react more to messages you receive with tingling on the legs. This is a sign of confirmation that the information you are receiving is good for you to follow up on. Also you may see bright shapes in front of you at times.

This is a sign of wellbeing for you, so do not be alarmed if you see them, especially at times when you least expect them. The synchronicity of events will also happen more often, bringing you joy in new awareness.

Please find out what your purpose is here in this lifetime before you read any further – that is, if you do not know already. Your purpose here is very important to you, for you to fulfil what you must do with it when you are multidimensional.

The role you are to play is vital and, as you have a unique talent, that will need to be put into use immediately. You are to work as you have been sent here to do. As we have said before, you can discover your true purpose by meditating every day, going to your higher or true self, who will give you the answers. If need be you can see a spiritual counsellor, who will help you discover what your purpose is. Spiritual counsellors are different to clairvoyants or mediums, who tell you what may happen in your future.

That can be fun as well as helpful, and predictions may or may not happen, as there is always free will involved. Spiritual counsellors are quite different in that they are guides to help you make your own decisions regarding your future, when you know your purpose and your true path in this lifetime.

They can access your guides and obtain information for you from them about yourself. Once you have opened up to channel yourself, you can access your own guides. So spiritual counsellors are facilitators for you to find your own answers.

When your channel is really open and you are receiving your own guidance, whether it be by clairaudience, clairvoyance, clairsentience or intuitive knowing, you will then be ready to do your major work of this lifetime.

Knowing you are finally doing what you are here to do will be such a relief to you, and you can relax and enjoy your time doing what you discover is the thing you really love.

Money

When you are absorbed in your true purpose, your money worries will no longer be an issue for you. When you are giving of yourself, the receiving of all you deserve will begin to happen for you.

There will be no need to make any effort to receive payment for your services. What you love doing you will do effortlessly, and that will be reward enough for using your unique talents to their greatest effect.

When you are all doing what you are here to do, money will no longer be of importance in the way it is now. Exchanging energies will be what it is all about.

Energy of the Sun

Energy is of utmost importance as we help you evolve to your highest level of spirituality. The energy you exchange with your family, friends, acquaintances and even the plants and animals is so very important. You are all made of energy and, depending on your thoughts, the energy will be more or less effective for you.

The more thoughts of pure love you use in your activities, the more pure energy you will give out to the world. The energy of the sun is of vital importance to you, being the grandest source of energy available.

When we have helped you to become multidimensional, you can receive all your supplies of energy from the sun. Food as you know it will no longer be necessary. In the meantime, if you can go in the sunlight every day, please do.

We do not want you to sunbake for long, as that will damage your skin. However a short while in the sun is very important to receive nourishment for your soul.

The winter in some countries is very severe, we know, and many of you have difficulty finding sunlight to be in. We suggest you visualise yourself on holiday when you meditate during your winter and think of yourself in the sun, even for a few minutes. The effect will be the same to your soul, and tide you over until the sun returns for you again.

Those of you who have abundant sunshine are very, very fortunate, and can enjoy the benefits always. Even so, you must respect the sun and not overdo your time in it.

The energy you receive from the sun can be used to greatest effect by transferring it to all you come in contact with, be it animal, plant or human. All will benefit from your loving giving of this precious gift. 'The sun will shine out of you', is a favourite saying of humans. Make it happen for you.

The next time you meet up with a friend who is looking radiant, please say to them 'The sun is shining through you', as that will be true for them, and you will be giving them confirmation of how well they are appearing to you. This will encourage them to continue to be positive with their life.

They know you are their friend and can help them continue to make their lives very fruitful and joyful. Your continual compliments to others will assist them to feel good about themselves, and your radiance will be a big boost to them to continue to take steps to discover their own life's purpose.

As we have said continuously, example is the only way you can help people to discover for themselves what they need to do to make their futures as exciting and joyful as yours will be. This is if you trust you are evolving, as you desire.

Many Tragedies now Happening

Much is being written in the popular press of many tragedies happening around the world. These will continue to happen for those who have not made the decision to begin a spiritual path to enlightenment.

Do not mourn for those who leave. They have made the choice for themselves to go and to begin again under different circumstances. They may not have succeeded in achieving their purpose here this time. You will be protected from tragedy if you have made the choice to walk the path to true enlightenment.

Some people are leaving the Earth plane now for other reasons. They are very enlightened ones whose work on the planet is complete, and they can continue their work from spirit more effectively.

We consider many of you had a knowing of this when such famous people as Diana, Princess of Wales, and Mother Theresa died in the same week. The impact on those left behind was very profound.

Their work was done and, in their going, they can have more impact. The reason for the worldwide mass mourning was a very complex one.

The masses were able to express their feelings openly 'en masse', not only for those who have gone, but also to express grief for their own issues that need to heal.

Being Honest with Yourself

As we have said earlier, your path to enlightenment will be very much easier if you are a very honest person, and that means firstly to be honest with yourself. You can not be an authentic person unless you know yourself to be who you really are meant to be.

Do you act differently with different people in your life? Do you react differently when you know that what the person is going to say to you may affect your point of view? We know it is not always easy to maintain your truth and to be consistent in your own way of being honest and truthful at all times.

Can you make a pact to be really honest with yourself when you need to make a choice of your view on a particular issue? Do not say or do what the majority may be saying or doing just to keep the peace. They may have made an incorrect judgement on the matter at hand, and not have the full facts at all.

Go with your heart always on making your decisions, and not from your head or logic. If you trust your heart or intuition, you will always be being true to yourself. It may not always seem the wisest choice in the short term; however, you will be so glad in the end that you have stuck with your choice of the heart. The wheel always turns full circle, and what may appear the wrong choice or hardest decision in the beginning may turn out to be the very wisest choice you could possibly have made.

Once you are honest with yourself, you will find it inevitably easy to always be honest with those you come in contact with. As you will always be telling the truth from your heart, you will not have any worries remembering what you said, or to whom.

Honest words will flow from you and you will find others are so very pleased to know you are genuine in all you say and do. All of the time you will then take on the aura of authenticity. You will emanate pure love and joy from your heart.

Those who come into your aura will feel loved, peaceful and happy when they are in your presence. Being honest with yourself and honest with others will bring you great rewards in your work and play.

You will bring energy to you which is progressive, exhilarating and very 'lucky'; by this we mean magnetic. You will draw to you the people who you will be able to learn with or from, or people who can give you information necessary for your advancement along your spiritual path. Events will occur which are major in your life, and crucial to your destiny.

The synchronicity will continue to amaze you, and we have no doubt you can have everything you desire if you respect and are always honest with yourself.

So many of you have great difficulty in realising how very special you are in the scheme of things; no one is less important than the next. You are all unique, and without you the world would be a lesser place.

Feelings

How wonderful you will feel when you know that all you say and do is the result of your feelings and not your logic. Feelings are all that you need to live your life. So very many humans shut down all their feelings and live like zombies; they do not allow access to them at all in case they have to face an issue.

Many of their blocked issues have been neatly tucked away for many years, and result from unresolved childhood experiences. When one deals with these issues at an adult level, you are free to move on in your evolution.

Every one of you has had a set of issues with which to deal, as that is why you are here on the Earth. The sooner you recognise your own issues and deal with them with wisdom, the sooner your life will become lighter, freer and more joyful.

The burden of unresolved issues is what causes illness and anxiety amongst you all. The minute you have resolved these problems, the sooner you can express your feelings without the fear of facing those issues which are hidden away.

You will no longer have any skeletons in your closet. Feelings are so very crucial in expressing your true self and in being honest with the true state of who you really are. Feelings of anger, feelings of fear and feelings of hate need to be acknowledged. Once you acknowledge which of these feelings you have, the sooner you can accept the reaction you have to the issue at hand and deal with it with knowledge and wisdom.

Childhood Traumas

Childhood traumas occur with everyone, and need to be resolved in adulthood before you can be a balanced, wise, loving human being.

No one escapes them, and it is not the trauma itself that is the issue – the handling or dealing with the issue is where the problems arise. When you can handle the issue with honesty and wisdom, you can then move on. If you, however, tackle the issue by pretending it never happened or you were not to blame, or pretending you were to blame but were not, you will need to go through the issue again.

As an adult you can reconcile where you went wrong in your dealing with the issue as a child.

This is a painful business and not easy to do, but it is so very necessary for you to move on in your life and then help others who have still to resolve their own issues.

So many children now have much inborn wisdom. They will not have the same issues to deal with in their adulthood. They will have very important work to do for the planet, as they will evolve very quickly and be able to get on with their tasks in this lifetime. Much will occur in the near future to confirm this view, and we know you will now be very alert to all signs of the new way of being in the world.

You are all needed to help transform the planet to the next stage of evolution. We must hurry to assist you in your own transformation and to be successful in bringing this about in the best way possible.

Enjoying Your Understanding

As you progress with all you are learning and understanding, so will your level of spirituality progress to the highest level possible for you.

You can then know you will indeed have no need to fear anything again, as your assurance is being given for attainment of all you desire and deserve as part of the human race.

As you are to be unconcerned with material things in the near future, enjoy making the most of all you have now. Do not hoard away your hard-earned money for the future, as in the future you will have no need for that kind of security.

Many people seem to be spending their time working so very hard to just exist and save for their retirement. They do not enjoy the now at all. All they can think of is having enough money to survive in their retirement.

Survive for what, we ask. If they have not developed a sense of spirituality, their lives are meaningless anyway, and they will not be here to have a retirement time at all. Therefore, enjoy yourselves. You have no need to put money away in superannuation funds, or scrimp and save and not give to others when they are in much need of your help now, and not in a few years' time. You will be unable to help them anyway, as you will have transformed to the multidimensional world of creative thought and love.

How exciting for you all to know the burden of the exchange of money for your services or for material possessions will soon be a thing of the past.

Energy exchange will be how the transactions take place. By that we mean that all of you will be using your unique gifts to help each other. Those of you who are healers will help those who are sick. Amongst those sick there may be a tradesman who can fix your plumbing or electricity, and others may have furniture you can have in exchange for your gift of healing.

As you will no longer need food or excess clothes as you may do now, you will have no need to buy these. People who have been involved in farming can help restore the land to its rightful way of being – natural forest and pasture – so that many can enjoy the beauty and solitude of those places again.

Rainbows of Colour

You may now experience many new ways of enjoying each other's company. The fun and laughter you may now enjoy will come to you in new ways. The time of sitting around a table to eat food and drink wine together will no longer need to be, so you can invent new ways of exchanging ideas with each other. This can occur in mind games, as you walk through the forests or play on the beaches.

Can you sit and imagine a rainbow of colour or many beautiful shapes of varying kinds? You can have fun guessing what they are, and what to do with them. Rainbows of colour are very vital to your mind-set now. By this we mean you are to be affected by the colours you see and the colours in the aura around you. Others will notice the colours of your aura so very easily when you are enlightened.

Depending on the colour of your aura for that moment in time, you will transmute energy out to those around you. They will detect this and be able to react in the way required, according to the colour you project. As they will also have a colour emanating from them, your colours will touch each other and create rainbows of colour that will benefit you all by your reactions to them at any particular time.

As you begin to understand the meaning of this, so the world will begin to vibrate very differently than now. We know this is to happen later on, and you have a while to wait for all this to occur. We just want you to know there are new ways of existing for you. Just because one sort of existence will be coming to an end, it does not mean the future is anything but exciting for all of you who are willing to walk the path to your best possible future.

Trust that all will be as it is meant to be.

New Fun and Games

The shapes you will see are forms of mathematical games for you to enjoy. As you will no longer need to eat or drink, you can extend your mind with guessing the connection between shapes and food and drinks.

This will be the substitute for your time-consuming passion with dining and conversing whilst doing so. The shapes of food and drink will be very pleasurable to you, even though you cannot imagine it being so from where you sit now.

The time will come, however, when you understand all of this, and you will be quite happy not to spend so much time buying, preparing, cooking, serving food and then clearing up afterwards.

We will be able to help you enjoy yourself in different ways as you evolve, as then you can spend much valuable time doing more important work for the planet and not spending time on unnecessary chores.

When you can, please sit quietly and think of all you have learnt so far in this text. Is your attitude very different now than when you began to read the book? We do hope so, as now we are ready for the final chapter, which will certainly expand your view of what is to now happen for you.

CHAPTER 6

The World Beyond Today

You have accomplished much on your path to your new beginning and may feel a very different human being. As you have been reading our words, you have developed many new awarenesses; your life will never be the same again.

We hope you are really excited about where you are journeying and look toward the future with much confidence and joy. As you will now know, your destiny is assured as long as you trust what you are doing, and trust in your guides to assist you in making correct decisions.

Enjoying and Understanding Your Guides

You really can have a lovely time with your spiritual guides. They usually have a great sense of humour and will tease you incessantly. They mean no harm to you and only want you to lighten up and take life less seriously.

Your guides do so hope you listen to their advice at all times. The ultimate decision is always yours, as you have free will. You alone are responsible for yourself and your destiny. Your guides are advisers, and will not interfere with what choices you make; however they will always be there.

They will help you celebrate if you have made a wise decision and be there to help you pick up the pieces if the decision you made was not a good one. You can see them shaking their heads just as your parents may have done when you were a child, when you chose unwisely. We know you need to learn the hard way sometimes.

Many of your guides are with you for specific purposes, as we have said before, and many of you will need to have a lot of help from many guides while you are evolving rapidly.

When you communicate with your own spiritual friends on an ongoing basis, you can be guided so much more specifically with your day-to-day lives.

Just remember not to take the advice of your guides literally or too quickly, as there may be a riddle or tease in what they are telling you. Please sit quietly for a while and think through the information you have been given; do some thinking of your own.

They may just be giving you a clue to the answer, or they may be telling you the opposite to what you really must do, as you need to realise what it is you really feel about a certain situation.

There may not be any consistency in the information you are given, and you must learn discernment in all you receive in the way of messages. It takes quite a while for you and your beautiful advisers to build up an understanding when you finally start to communicate on a two-way level.

Previously the communication has been a one-way transfer of ideas from your guides to you, and at last you have realised you can communicate back to them. You need to learn a language you both understand.

This may take many months, with continuous practice. As you begin to feel comfortable with each other and you have sorted out a language you understand, then your real work can begin.

When you are at last very good at communicating with your wise friends, you will be able to find direction more easily for your own life and for those close to you. You will be able to assist them in finding out their life purpose and also help them develop their own spirituality.

We cannot guarantee you or they will have happier lives. That is up to you and your free will. All we can do is help you to make wiser decisions based on information you receive from your guides.

They will always wish the best for you and know what may happen for you if you act on those wise decisions. Sometimes, however, you need to learn hard lessons and you choose unwisely. Then you may certainly have uncomfortable experiences that take you off your path for a while, before you get back on track again.

You will then learn to trust your guides more for the information they are giving you. Of course at times they may tell you the opposite to what you really should do, and this makes life confusing for you.

However, usually the advice given in that instance will be the easy solution and very apparently the wrong one. You will be encouraged to think about it deep down, and you just know you must not accept the easy way out.

Much can be said for waiting for answers to come to you, and this involves patience and often lonely times while you sort through your various options. Time sorts out a lot of decisions for you.

Even though we have no time here, we know you have linear time in the physical world, which is very important at times when you are waiting for the right answers to come.

We see events occurring when the circumstances are right, and we are not able to tell exactly when it is for you. We see only that when one set of circumstances arrives, they will trigger off other things happening for you and those around you.

So have patience, and always follow your heart and not your head. You will then find things do work out for you always.

Strange Events

Towards the new beginning now coming for all of you, you will notice many strange events beginning to occur in your life.

These may be strange smells around you, music being turned on without any explanation, impulses to go to a certain place only to find a favourite friend there, or animals coming to you out of the blue. Accept all these strange happenings with good grace. Know your guides are making sure you know they are with you always.

Man–Woman Relationships

We have not spoken about man–woman relationships so far and so now we can explain to you what the circumstances may be.

In the future, men and women will no longer form partnerships for life. As strange as this may seem, men and women will have no need or want to be together always with the same person, as has happened in the past. As the new beginning evolves, men and women will come and go in their relationships, coming together when the time is right for them to be together, and then parting company when the circumstances change. Now you are more enlightened, you will realise that having a partner forever by your side is not really necessary. Being well balanced yourself, you can have many friends for varying reasons, and at different stages of your life.

Men and women are certainly needed to be together to procreate and to be nurturing parents for their offspring, and we certainly condone that. You may, however, in other circumstances, be better off being a free spirit and being able to have a few different relationships, perhaps all at the same time and for diverse experiences, as long as no harm is done to any of you in the way of co-dependency.

By this we mean you must not have any expectations of each other, and just enjoy each other's company at that very time you are together, not expecting anything more of them.

You will be so very pleased to understand what we mean by this is not to be madly having many love affairs all at once.

What we mean is to be discerning and mature about your chosen relationships and respect the other people with whom you are involved, with all your heart.

You will find much happiness when you do not expect anything from them – only have expectations of yourself, and that is to live with respect for yourself always, doing only what you honestly believe is very acceptable to your own soul and not accept anything less.

Soul Mates

We know you each have many soul mates around you, who come and go in your lives when they are needed by you. So just because one of them has gone from your life, even for a while, does not mean you must not be friendly or intimate with another of your soul mates, who may appear in your life at that time.

You may ask, how is one to know if a person is truly a soul mate. Please sit very quietly and think very deeply about this, as your soul mates will always seem to you as though you have known them forever, even when you first meet them.

You will just have an inner knowing about them, and feel so very comfortable in their energy space. By soul mate we mean others of your soul group who come from the same matter or part of the universe. You are part of the same family of matter and so instantly feel comfortable with each other, as you have known them from other times and will know them forever.

We suggest you now explore your spirituality as much as you can with people you come across, remembering you must not try to change their thinking by force – just show them by example what you are doing and how you are living your life.

You will be amazed how often you sow the seed in others' minds to have a little look at all they have been denying in themselves for so long. You can influence so many without realising it.

You will only help the world when you give out your knowledge to those ready to receive. As you can picture, with you all leading your lives so very differently from now, the world in a few years' time will begin to transform.

The Rising of the Seas

The transformation beginning to occur now is very subtle in the difference it will make in the near future. As time goes on, the changes will become more evident, with many obvious changes to everything and everyone. The seas are to rise quite dramatically and cover much of the lower lands of the world.

We suggest you relocate to higher levels if you live near the coast, to well above the present level of the ocean. Many cities will be covered with water and many people will lose their properties. It will be a good idea to sell up and move early so you are not caught with a property that is not saleable. By this we mean to go before the panic sets in.

The best time to move inland is by early in this new century. We cannot guarantee your safety if you disregard this advice. This applies to all countries of the Northern Hemisphere, as well as some in the Southern Hemisphere, such as Australia, New Zealand, South Africa and South America.

The northern parts of the Southern Hemisphere will not be affected, as they are to escape the impact of the rising waters for reasons to be made known later. We need to explain to you not to be alarmed totally, as these warnings have been told before and you can rest assured we are only adding to information already available.

You may ask why are the seas to rise up and flood the lands. We now wish to explain to you why.

The Earth is becoming warmer due to the hole in the ozone layer. This is being enlarged with the pollutants created by mankind polluting the vital layers of the Earth. Icebergs are to melt and so the sea levels will rise and create a much more vast ocean, which will take over more of the surface of the planet.

Also, the axis of the Earth is slowly moving to another angle, and this will create a shift in the position of the waters of the world. The time is now coming for humankind to reconsider their place on the Earth plane.

Humans have always taken what they need from the Earth, and very few have respected the need to put back and compensate for what has been taken. As many of you know, man has mined the Earth – and this is perfectly acceptable as long as respect is given to the place from where the minerals are removed, and love and gratitude are given.

If mankind continues to take and not be grateful, the planet Earth will no longer be in balance.

This is why mankind needs to have major events happening such as the global warming and big shakeups in habitat – to make sure man respects his home. Can you understand this now? We are only giving you signs to ask you to respect the Earth continuously.

The time is now here for this major signal to you all and, as the seas rise, those in control of industry will reconsider the damage accrued that caused these changes to take place.

We consider the human race will have more respect as these changes occur. We are very aware these changes will be very slow to happen, and you are in reality to have ample warning.

The need to move will be a very significant decision for you all, and we do urge you to make the move away from low-lying coastal areas soon.

Many of you may be upset by this need to leave the edge of the landmass where you may now live, as living by the water is the very best possible place to be for your spiritual enlightenment.

We do understand this requirement of yours, and so we need to explain that you can also receive much wonderful nurturing from the forests and lakes in the interior of a landmass. These areas are very beautiful also, and until the change has occurred we do suggest you relocate to areas of great beauty inland.

Can you now relax, watch for the signs of change coming, and move when you are ready to move naturally? Those of you who need to remain will still have ample warning and not be caught suddenly. Your guides will alert you to the very best time for you to leave.

The reasons the northern part of the Southern Hemisphere will escape this flooding will be due to the way the axis of the Earth will tilt to a new angle, as we have said. The angle will favour this area of the landmasses.

You may be wondering why we are spending so much time telling you about this issue to come into your lives if you live near the coast.

The fact that so much of the world's population lives near the oceans is the very reason we wish to explain the huge disasters that will occur if you are all located there when the seas rise.

If you move away at the last moment, the infrastructure of inland cities and towns will not be able to cope with the mass exodus of millions of people to their cities, even over a period of months. This is why we suggest many of you must move soon, to arrive gradually in the more suitable locations.

On the whole, the planet will become much smaller with its land-masses and larger with its ocean masses. Survival in the three-dimensional world will depend on you living on higher ground, i.e. at higher altitudes, with all communications by rail and road needing to be revised, as many systems will be under water.

By becoming multidimensional you will be able to avoid all of the chaos. You can move to other dimensions, taking your body with you, and returning when the chaos has disappeared and those left on the Earth plane have learnt valuable lessons in their spiritual evolution due to what has happened to them.

Your body will dissolve for the time you are in other dimensions – by this we mean the energy vibrations will alter and so your physical body will not be apparent, or have the same properties as it usually has. When you wish to return in the physical form again, the energy vibrations will reassemble in the correct manner for your body to be physical again.

We emphasise this to all who listen. Please do not linger too long at the coast or, if you do, do not own property there, as it will be of no value to you when the waters come.

As you prepare to leave the coastline, if that is where you live, take a few moments to inform others of the changes coming and explain why they need to consider going higher up into the hills to live, and not stay at the coast. Those of you who live inland can explain to your relations and friends who live on the coast to move away early in this new century.

This is all part of the plan for the future of your new world to come. Many of you are becoming beautifully enlightened, and, by practising what we have suggested, you can relax and enjoy your feelings of joy and happiness. Trust you will be guided in your choice of new abode, if it is necessary.

Living in Many Dimensions

The next phase of your new beginning will be when you are regularly moving through many dimensions as you live your physical life. The new way of living your life will be with a different set of patterns of daily habits. For example, instead of sleeping for as long as you do in a bed, you will tend to take off into another dimension where you can enjoy all the lovely happenings with your friends in other parts of the planet. Instead of having to get on a plane to go and visit them, you can visit them at will in another dimension without even leaving home. You may think this strange now; however it will really begin to happen for you very easily when the time is right. The ability to teleport at will, consciously and unconsciously, will be easy for you whenever you wish. You will still go to sleep for a time in your bed, connecting with your soul mates at that time, as it is very important for us to connect with the real you every night.

Much will come in the next few years to help with your spiritual progress, and you can rest assured that you will never be alone in your quest for attaining enlightenment.

We are to be with you always, and the more you acknowledge us the quicker will be your evolution. The monotony of daily lives will be no longer, as your access to multidimensional reality will give you much greater freedom with your spirit to explore so much more of other realities.

We do hope you look forward to these times with excitement, as we know you will enjoy your physical lives so very much more. The new beginning will be very satisfying and rewarding for you all.

The time is now here for you to become the very person you truly are, and that is a person of great authenticity, a person of great love for all including yourself, and a person who has great trust in an existence beyond the three-dimensional reality.

The world beyond today is a greater world of many realities, and, as you explore these incredibly wondrous realities, you will discover your own uniqueness as a soul who is beyond time and space. You will have the ability to live in realities that encompass many new and, until now, unknown avenues for you to exist.

Please remember our messages in these words, as the steps towards your new beginning are very easy and very necessary for the future of the planet. You can now go and help all those you meet to begin their journeys towards the world beyond today.

Your future is yours to choose. You can be the bringer of love, wisdom and joyfulness to all you encounter. As you live each day with love and light, you can be all that you desire.

We give you great love and blessings.
The messengers from Illanitis

Epilogue

I wish now to share with you, dear reader, the many tests and trials I have experienced during my own journey towards enlightenment. Many of them have been humorous and enjoyable, and some have helped me learn hard but valuable lessons.

As my spiritual friends have said, you will have many experiences that will help you to become aware of your guides' presence, and you need to understand what you are learning on your new spiritual journey. At times I have been very much in awe of the magic of spirit, and have been left wondering how I could ever have not noticed the presence of my guides in all those years preceding my new-found knowledge and understanding.

Armed with my new knowledge and my ability to write with my guides, I have been presented with many situations with which I have needed to deal.

The first of these was when I was told very early in my writing that I would need to travel to the United States of America to be with my son Digby, as he was to have a serious car accident and badly injure his leg. He was at the time exploring South America with a girlfriend, and would be journeying through the United States of America and on to Canada in a few months' time.

This information was presented to me on a regular basis over many weeks, and I was instructed not to tell Digby of the impending accident, as he needed to have it for his own growth. With great restraint, I kept this information to myself and prepared for the phone call I thought must come to inform me of the accident on the date that I had been given.

On the day prior to this date, I was writing with my guides Hanka and Manilong and asked, with a thumping heart, was I still to be ready to go to America the next day when the phone call came with this awful news. The message I received was that it was no longer necessary for me to go, as I had passed their test of trust by not informing Digby and by being prepared to believe what they had told me. It was all a mind game!

A few moments after this information was given to me, the phone rang. It was Digby ringing to say he and his girlfriend had arrived safely in Canada. The timing of that call was incredible.

On two separate occasions I have been tested very severely, when I have had encounters with undesirable people.

On the first occasion I very unwisely allowed a young man to enter my home to help me with protecting myself from mischievous spirits. An unsuspecting friend had given my phone number to him, as she thought he would alleviate my concerns about the negative spirits that might possibly be around me.

Not only was this man a fraud, his intent was to shut down my channel, as he had done to others. He was really a messenger from the dark who envied the opening up of so many people. Very fortunately I realised his intent early enough to send him away with unconditional love.

Perhaps he has now seen the light. I certainly learnt a very valuable lesson that day.

The other occasion was when an angry, negative client came at the insistence of a very lovely lady. She was very upset about her position in life and, although she knew what she must do, insisted on trying to find an easy way out.

When the message came through to her in the writing on the wisest action to take for her highest good, she rejected the guidance and left with a very negative attitude.

I felt very vulnerable and sad for her. She left me with a feeling of negativity. Instead of ridding myself of negative energies by visualising them leaving my home, and then visualising white light around everything, I allowed the negativity to remain in the atmosphere.

That night my car was stolen (due to the negative energy) and then found abandoned a few streets away. Luckily no major damage was done, and two wonderful young men, Adrian and Darren, were able to repair it for me very inexpensively.

I know that they were sent to me as a thankyou from my spiritual guides. It was a thankyou for going through the test, as that is what it was. It was another test – to see how I would react to negativity. Although I had felt vulnerable while with the client, I had stayed calm and loving towards her and sent her away with much love and understanding.

From that day on I have always put a circle of white light around myself, my home and my car as a protection against negativity.

One of my saddest experiences was as follows. Six months before a very beautiful man friend of mine died, I had warning of his death in my writing. I had only been writing for two months at that stage. I was not asking for protection for myself, as I would have been wise to do, to protect negative energies appearing in my writing, even though all had been well until this particular day.

During my conversation in my daily writing I was told of my friend's collapse, and later in the day I received the information that he had died. I went through incredible trauma at this news, as he and I were the real true loves of each other's lives, even though it was no longer appropriate for us to be living together as we had done previously.

No one rang me to confirm the news. The pain of his supposed going was incredibly difficult for me to cope with, and I battled with my emotions for quite some time before ringing his sister to inquire after him. I felt it very difficult to explain my information source to his family or friends.

To my relief I discovered he was still very much alive and happy. I then went back to ask Hanka and Manilong why they had told me of his death.

Their reply was to inform me that mischievous guides had 'got in' through the 'cracks'. I quickly learnt to always protect myself before writing. When my dear friend did indeed physically die nearly six months later – on the tennis court of a heart attack – I realised it had also been my preparation for his impending departure.

When he did die, my ability to 'speak' with him only a few hours later alleviated all traumas for me, and we have discussed the reasons for our magnificent union of souls in this lifetime. He is now able to offer me much wise advice from the spirit world, and I know he is always with me.

His name was John, he is now my guide, and we certainly are closely connected, as we were when he was with me in the physical form.

I wish to explain that it is very necessary to have a little ritual to protect yourself from negative and mischievous spirits when you first begin to communicate with the spirit world.

The important part is in the intention behind what you say in your ritual. This will keep away all undesirable spirits. As your vibrations rise to a higher level, your purity and lightness will naturally protect you.

Another event in my spiritual growth was when one night there was supposedly a fire that was burning outside my apartment.

I smelt smoke and my guides had me hurrying out to check, only to find they had sent me outside to take a look at the magnificent night sky and all the stars. It was a hot summer evening, and I had been inside reading. I loved the trick they played on me.

My guides mentioned to you about animals possibly coming into your life out of the blue. One day, while I was writing and talking with them, they told me to watch out for a black cat that would come into my life. To begin with it would be Hanka's spirit in the cat.

The very next day I went walking near where I live and a black cat came up to me in the street. It rubbed itself against my legs, even allowing me to pick it up.

It was a most wonderful confirmation of what I had been told. Gradually over the next few weeks the cat, after seeing where I lived, began to visit me.

Eventually I had the regular company of this beautiful cat, which was very comforting when John died a few weeks later, and for the nine months afterwards while grieving for him.

Of course my thoughtful and caring guides had arranged the presence of the cat for me in advance.

Now this wonderful animal has died, after also being of assistance to other people living nearby. He was taken to the veterinary doctor with meningitis, on the first anniversary of John's death, and put down on the anniversary of his funeral. The cat's work was over!

The very nature of miracles had been evident one morning previously when I was having my breakfast outside in my sunny courtyard with the contented, loyal black cat sitting near me. Suddenly we heard something land on the large umbrella above my head. As nothing was to be seen, I went on eating breakfast while thinking this was a rather unusual happening. Then we heard something hit the shrubbery behind me, although again there was nothing to be seen. I continued on with my breakfast, and again we heard something land on the umbrella, but this time fall from it onto the paving near the table. It was a little rock. On investigating further, I discovered another small rock on the top of the umbrella. This was very strange, as there was no evidence of anyone nearby who could have thrown them. How did they come?

A few hours later I was visiting friends, one of whom is a shaman. He gave me a message from spirit: Did I have enough rocks in my pocket and was I weighed down enough? He said this to me without knowing I had received two rocks 'from the sky' only a few hours earlier.

When I returned home I asked in my writing for an explanation of this extraordinary gift. Archangel Michael explained to me that the rocks (representing the earth) were manifested as a gift to me to assist me to ground myself after communicating with spirit, to bring me back into three-dimensional reality and into connection with the earth.

The receiving of these rocks was certainly a miraculous manifestation, showing miracles happen with magical ease when necessary.

So you can see, dear reader, perhaps life will never be the same again for you now you are opening up to spirit. Please enjoy every moment of your life and know, with your new awareness, that every day can be an exciting challenge and a rewarding adventure.

My blessings to you all!
Merriene

Merriene Scott welcomes your correspondence.
Please contact her at
Email: merriene@merrienescott.com
www.merrienescott.com

About the Cover

The subject of this 'wildflower mandala', which was created for the book by Jen McCathie, is the tiny flower of the wild potato bush. Jen used a macro photograph to create the mandala by reversing and repeating the original image.

She was seeking to express what she sees through the lens: the inherent rhythm and design, balance and harmony, in nature. This inspires in her feelings of gratitude, which she finds well expressed in these words by Joanna Macey in her book *Coming Back to Life*:

'We have received an inestimable gift. To be alive in the beautiful, self-organising universe – to participate in the dance of life with the senses to perceive it, lungs that breathe it, organs that draw nourishment from it – it is wonder beyond words.

'As it is, moreover, an extraordinary privilege to be accorded a human life, with this self reflective consciousness which brings awareness of our own actions and the ability to make choices, it lets us choose to take part in the healing of our world.'